The Stammering Man

Ian McEwen

Templar Poetry

First Published 2010 by Templar Poetry

Templar Poetry is an imprint of Delamide & Bell

Fenelon House

Kingsbridge Terrace

58 Dale Road, Matlock, Derbyshire

DE4 3NB

www.templarpoetry.co.uk

ISBN 978-1-906285-97-5

For permission to reprint or broadcast these poems write to Templar Poetry

A CIP catalogue record of this book is available from the British Library.

Typeset by Pliny
Cover: lino cut by James Weir
Printed and bound in India

Acknowledgements

Acknowledgements are due to the editors of publications in which some of the poems in this pamphlet first appeared, *Seam, Iota, Poetry Wales* and *Poetry Review*. 'Terwick Mill 1944' was included in the Flarestack competition anthology *Mr Barton Isn't Paying*. 'Alter' was included in the Cinnamon Press anthology *The Visitors*.

Contents

Tube

The carriage grates out of Moorgate.
I hang on, jammed between two Suns
    and a Daily Express - You Are What You Eat -   trumpets The World's Greatest Newspaper
                which maybe is not very true but   I grab on to these dirty strap-lines -
            infectious — you are who you shag - you are what you drive - you are what   you read: the parrot instinct makes
                                        you chant - in the clanky music of   the train a risky slalom between
                            headphones and the shiny posters   the rhythms that bang in the head
                                                            the parallel slang of the tracks
                                                            the cliché of clackety-clacks
                                                            the slap of the slack of the facts.

Alter

Don't you think
of your double
out in the rain
he's staring through?
Shrugged up
on closed-circuit,
grainy, half-shrouded.
He's outside when you're
in: it's him that
changed the alarm
as you slept. He
uses your mug,
his wet steps
the sound effect
that trails you home,
cloth and bone
golem of code,
his fuzzy tones
on the entry-phone.
It's his palm mark
wounded with drops
on the window,
inside the house,
as you fumble
the lock, it's him,
listen and watch.

As you fumble,
out in the rain
that trails you home,
on closed circuit
wounded with drops,
listen and watch:
the sound effect
of your double
on the entry-phone,
his wet steps
in. It's him, that
golem of code.
As you slept he
changed the alarm,
uses your mug.
He's outside when you're
inside the house,
shrugged up,
his fuzzy tones
grainy, half-shrouded
cloth and bone.
It's his palm mark
on the window.
He's staring through
the lock, its him,
don't you think?

2

A Tessellation

1

The story paces itself just right
for the nightly bulletin: the fire, the vanished
   family, the slow investigation hampered by the cryptic 'conditions of the site'
    by hourly conferences, camera lights shots of the burned out stables and garages
     time to speculate – amplified while the bodies, high-tented like the fete, hold back   their names. There's a lot of interest in the pets
        details, the 'three luxury cars' that are 'reduced to charcoal', to fossil imprints,
        X-rays of themselves. Excited we guess like it's a quiz – night by night at ten
          the nation salivates, the newsreader
          knows she has them now, tight focus,
          the story just right for her talent.

2

All this in the press – how the husband, father
must have shot, small calibre, up close,
the wife, the daughter – so that next to me a stranger, reading the same thing in a different paper
    leans across the cash desk: Isn't it terrible?   Do the details mesh? We play detectives
   Could he? Did they? – and what bothers us most is to find out that money, repossession, made all this, what? sadness, self-hate, anger?
        weightless entries in some drab office made this man, this 'expert in fire-safety'
        set it all off, to a plan, a script made him wear his own design of vest
          to walk back in, over the keyed blocks
          of the drive, made him make the pieces fit.

The Trial of the Stammering Man

1.   *The arrest of the stammering man*

say hello to the stammering man
and he will smile back, when
you ask him the way to the station
he wants to oblige, he points – then

say hello to the stammering man
really he can't hurt a fly
he cannot say why
he can't even say 'shoo'
he gets stuck on the horrors
the one-way NO ENTRY

say hello to the stammering man
don't be nervous or shy
he wants to be kind
he can't finish the job
don't finish it for him
he works and he works at
his Antarctic map for a path
for a roundabout path.

2.   *The charges*

the stammering man has
a car that won't start
and his Hoover is blocked

the stammering man has
an analogue life
it sticks in the groove
it jams in the gate
when he talks to his wife

the stammering man has
a fear of the blank
like a stick-man cartoon
it won't move it can't move
in the flick-book of strife
he's all frozen up. He starts
and he starts but he cannot B-B-B

3. *The stammering man confirms his name*

The stammering man has got
to climb G. Guttural, Glottal   Gonadotrophin
Global, G-G-G- Goorr-   Gladiolus   G-G-G
Green, Glass, Greasy   Garage
Geometric, Gerontocratic

4. *The stammering man instructs counsel*

                                                     when mouth and soul are
                    such sense as attain to   when salt and throat are
but rarely the soul is   such sense as is able   when sore and red are
but rarely the sense is   as able as soul to   when rose and throat are
the throat is but rarely as able the soul to   when sense and rose are
                    such sense as attain to   when soul and sore are
                                         when sense and throat are

5. *The stammering man enters a plea*

                                  G-G-G
                    G-G-G   says the stammering man
G-G-G   in the box on the dock   G-G-G
says the stammering man   G-G-G   but his voice won't unlock
G-G-G   as the terminal phlegm   like a cork on his thought
like an overblown reed   in his throat G-G Gathers   B-B Blocks
                    T-truth punches his nose   G-G-G
                                       N-Not Innocent.

6.   *He gives his evidence*

If words are the bergs
and they're 9/10 submerged   and they're cold and so slick
they float and they hurt   with the mass of a ship oh he'd love them to stop
when they clam in the throat   and he can't get a grip oh he'd stop them to love   but they close and they lock.
when they jam in the head   all blinded and white   but they close and they lock
and they puncture the boat   when they close and they lock
and they close and they lock

7.   *Theories presented in mitigation*

Physical trauma at birth (Monroe, 1954). Not wired normal (Dicker, 1978). Expectation. Being told to 'take a breath' (Churchill, 1930). Lysosomal variants. Stress such as moving, the birth of a sibling (Palin, 1987). genetic in origin (Drayna, 2009). A sudden growth in linguistic ability (Carlyle, 1843). Fear. Basal ganglia (Molt, 1999). Parental reaction. Encephalitis (Sahli, 1920). Being told to slow down (Bevan, 1945). Anxiety told to speak clearly. Dual premotor systems (Alm, 2005). Told to say it again. Traumatic experience as in bereavement (Buber, 1947). Psychogenic reaction to physical trauma. Tumour and fear. Stroke. Drug abuse. Increased activation of the right hemisphere (Balls, 2010). Auditory processing differences (Carroll, 1865). Unusual neurodevelopment (Demosthenes, 350BCE).

We don't stammer when we sing.

8.   *The Midas of Ice*

the stammering man is trapped in his floe   each way he looks is alternative glass
its fractures and flaws grab his words   with a deepening blue that holds tight
he tries to pick verbs, they freeze before he can send any onward or back   every pickaxe and auger, the meters   with intricate wires and black boxes
packed solid with crystals of snow say again and again what he cannot   read off the scale, locked to the stops   that crack like a prayer that he cannot
quite catch as they ram and they ring   of this beautiful trauma
as they score up the face of the world   that shores up the face of the world

9.   *The joke's on the stammering man*

The stammering man walks into a bar
and orders a drink.
He does not stammer.
He cannot blink.

Barnacle or Brent

                                                                                         crank

branta   lever
  anser   hinge
    fulcrum   sky spall
      creaky   salt scale
        hinge   scrape
          crank   delta
            lever   plaint
              awl to   tin
                carve   of heaven
                  the can

The One-Stop Shop

For all the essentials – milk, bread, sausage
rolls, fluorescent bags of sweets and
a shelf full of porn   marshmallow arcs of pink
just visible through the milky plastic,   though I don't think that's why they call it soft:
it's sat above the racks on cars and gardens,   the opaque glaze is there for modesty   at the till or for the other shoppers
or so the clientele must go as far as   purchasing that last ingredient, queuing up
to pay. There's no sign of embarrassment   and they are only pictures, after all, of the real,
a bit re-touched, and my son at 10 never
even has to ask 'Dad, what are they all for?'

Footpath

The grass pummelled
here, stems combed, mud beaten
to the surface, a pubic wedge, pointer   not North or East or West but
    of turns and lumps, a change of spoor   animal habit that turns burnished
        as it encounters stubble,   the urgent lazy call of history,   this is the custom, the route we go,
                self-unpacking, a duct into   a scale model of our way through
           unplanned muddled landscape, the good and evil hawthorn bowers
                              that overrun their bones, frothy,
                                  dull-white, musked of hospital.

Cut

A track mark of gutted storage, arse-ends
of building, weed-fractured wharves,
toothless gates and hacked-out windows,   purple sockets without the strength to mend
the canal runs a liquid bruise through town,   the past, the gross national product,
    that nobody talks to or looks at except the local winos, and one hunched kid   he's carbonised, black jeans, black hoody
                sat on his fishing kit, beside his supplies,   black roach pole, tapered to nylon, impaled
                    maggots, that gesture as they drown: bait. He flicks out more writhing pearls
                                and picks a rip of living silver,
                                    sharp, from the livid water.

The Wind Farms

Isn't it Tibet or somewhere they use
wheels for prayer? What open arms
they have, what whiteness and patience   - something we'd all like from time to time -
and isn't it an exercise of spirit   this form of stasis they achieve
the attempt to keep the world still   by turning? If it really all goes wrong,   these slow gyroscopes
                                will they be all that shows? Up to their hips   baptising each tip in turn
                                in water, hailing unintelligent life,   the best things left, waving goodbye
                                                    or hello as they roll the horizon
                                                    and diligently plough the wind.

Eye

There's a remark about a painter
(Monet I think) being just an eye,
        so maybe call this just   an angle, a place to look from
    a voice – perhaps a voice that   wears limits, must show horizons
    has too much 'I' in it. But then whatever I climb, unfair to point at 'you'   to take the mantle for 'us' for 'we'
                to claim like a magician nothing's hidden   or to prestidigitate with 'she' and 'he'
                    swirling a black and crimson cape   those silks that pull the gaze away
                                        from the trick, so 'they' take an eye
                                        off the cup, the rope, the local ball.

After Hitchens

1. Terwick Mill No.11 (Early Autumn 1944)

old England dabbed lead headed under the clouds' long decrescendo
browned off and patched trees chipped with light, the air pure empty
out of action: the pattern that is cut of heraldic movement, antisolar,
still in fatigues, as hands break across a cavity of static bronze, so
ten more ration years, marginal pools bulge in forward weight, far
off earth holds the slow lapsed forms, demands this serious anatomy
in pigment, vowels of ground water, that pour and pours a liquid ray
as crushed, struggled over and over in situ low amorphous dough

2. Standing Nude (1971)

Echo and the pulse of shadow
onto light as the halo by her hair
is bent and calls the neck supple
how tender space is the body waves
of the body where shoulders turn
and draw on upward through earth
the friction of depth in rubbed
rose nipple for height the rusted
arm pulls back from the apple
green-wash of belly that made
that makes from emerald fall
a gravity all folded on the dark
cut and the lovely pendulum
thus soft and umber in the bulk
for so commands the figure of
its ground as the knee measures
perspective on inflected space
laid at her feet ochre and black

3. In the Garden (1979)

part   tone and line and colour music   cobalt violet: the spaces left   between the verticals of trees   temper all

say   cut open by the musical   manganese blue: a fairly clear idea of what has to be done   the movement must

see   gesture, because the body is music   cadmium red: though never clear how, painted to be listened to   pass clear

hear rhythm and chord, the musical   titanium   drawing left behind, grown out of   through the arm, off-spinning light

turn   skin of colour. Only music   white or zinc white: the receding plane of the lake, the canvas claims   bent to the eye

draw   to parse the light, the musical cadmium yellow: tree, sky, ragwort: a white house surrounded   by the water of music

hold   breath that measures through music cobalt blue: an upright of flowers: orange days through and through and through

Scape

Schadenfreude. Shady joy – more – glee
    today as markets crash and bankers,
    boys who thought the fast and polished   bonus-laden, infinite future
    path was solid, hear it shatter. They file   chastened, chastised,
    whey-faced through the glass doors. Their   progress latches on to salvage   in a black ant-chain of purpose
        laden with plants, bars from the vender: just last week, the seventh year
        we put our mourning on parade   the minister is sober, he cashes in both
        ways. Streams and streams of people,
        ashen, ash, ashes.

The Comic

I thought he was dead already, but no
it happened last night: ninety one and broke
in Eastbourne – the kind of place he'd set   his comedy of stereotype and error,
   double-entendre skits. The stations offer   stock characters, slightly embarrassing
     dead-pans that talk 'craft' and praise   clips of shows: his grainy music hall   arms flung far too wide for the TV screen,
         mannerisms - half the act - and laughing,   jerking the shoulders, a paroxysm,
           laughing fit to bust at his own joke,   so much sometimes, often, that we never hear
                               the punch-lines, but such shaking - infectious
                                 spasms - this choking Calvary of laughter.

The Answer

That's it — she's blown it — picked the wrong
one and lost out on the big prize. The TV
host extends his arms, elbows bent,   palms up toward the contestant,
maybe in a kind of blessing,   a half-apology/half-celebration
- and he is a saint,   outlined in azure, the light full-on   centre-stage, he offers something,
as we go to the commercial break,   something on another channel,
he means: hey, you got this far!   and gives this universal second prize,
this catch-all dismissal-cum-appeal-cum
-unfinished-hug. You will see it all the time.

The Sandwich-Board Passion

Outside the Odeon there used to stand
the sandwich-board Jeremiah - REPENT
 in red block letters. He, black book in hand,   his body shocked at every consonant,
   flowed and swayed to the same words, almost   a puppet, dangled on a filament of heaven,
      the same over and over THE LORD IS NIGH: twenty years might still count nigh enough   on God's clock as it ticks down the planet
                                          to whatever he believed in and I don't   to some last feature of smoke and fire,
                                           his every word a jerk of the hands   a flickery smudge like a silent film.
                                                                                       He was really high and there's just
                                                                                       one movie rule for that:

                               DON'T LOOK DOWN.

blue

blue   fire   fire   blue   fire   blue   fire   fire blue   fire   blue   blue

fire   blue   blue   blue   fire   blue   fire   fire   blue   blue fire   blue

breath spire   breath spire   breath space   breath spire   restless   blue

over   tireless blue   eye finds no restlose place   breath stretch spire breath   to blue   more   race blues

into   blue on blue pire   past   sight breaks   in   restless   blue outpace   spires of blue blue space   breathe

in   through   over   alephs   breath spire   breath spire

gulf of   blue fire over   blue breath   blue space   blue tireless

blue wraith   the gulf   height   breaks in   and over   blue   suspires

blue   leapfrogs over   vast   spires   of   restless blue   eye loses   no rest stretch

chase   blue alephs   lost   in blue fire   overturn in blue vaults in   a gulf of   blue

of light   aspire   the eye   does not see loses   grip as   fresh alephs

on blue expires in blue   stretches over   and over all the orders

stretches climbs over higher leaps blue

up blue over blue breath

over and face

day turn

One

Cloudless

Mud

The toddler, feet splayed, still at the duck-
  walk stage, flippers away from her –
  It's a test, a push against the bubble   the surface tension of the mother's look
  he lives in. He's found the one wet puddle left unfocused now, gathering the leaf rubble
    in the park – a muddy canvas. He squats -   he presses one blue rubber shoe in   - admires the sculpted riddle
                  then the fingers dabble, the whole hand deliberately as any potter
                  pulls up a wall of clay. He wobbles lifts slubber to his mouth and – *No*
                                     the mother bawls – glares: we're in trouble
                                   now. Obdurate, we ball it, thumb it, rub it in.